Stuck in Neutral

Stuck in Neutral
stories

Barbara Wood

Stuck in Neutral: Stories
Copyright © 2012 by Barbara Wood

Cover design by Rita Petithory
Author photos by Upstate Photographers
Book design by Melissa Mykal Batalin

Printed in the United States of America

The Troy Book Makers • Troy, New York • thetroybookmakers.com

To order additional copies of this title, contact your favorite local
bookstore or visit www.tbmbooks.com

ISBN: 978-1-61468-074-1

*This book is dedicated
to my beautiful family and friends
who brighten and fill my life,
and to my late parents who
encouraged me in everything I tried
except, possibly, the violin.
I love you all.*

Thanks

Many thanks to my friends for their invaluable help with this book:

Lucia Nevai, for her expertise in editing, and being a great writing teacher,

Rita Petithory, for her amazing graphic design talents, and

Jaime Walton, for the wonderful cover photograph, which inspired me to finish this project.

• • •

Thank you to the oysters in my life who planted the tiny seeds of irritation which grew into my pearls of wisdom. Without you, I wouldn't be adorned by my necklace of enlightenment.

To R., as promised, thanks for the angst.

Contents

Stuck in Neutral

Stuck in Neutral

My exterior is shiny, with no more than the usual number of dents, dings, and scratches, considering the age of the vehicle, which is gently used but has never been pre-owned. My upholstery is clean, with only a few spots and snags, and a little sagging in the seat. The tank is full, the engine is revving, and here I am, stuck in neutral. Despite my need and desire to move, I cannot seem to go forward, do not want to go in reverse, and continue to sit here, waiting and waiting, unable to continue on my journey.

When I moved from a two-car garage, to a one-car, I heeded all the signs. I drove out carefully, yielded when I had to, pausing at the new crossroads in my life, carefully looking left and right, checking my mirrors and blind spots, to decide which direction to take. There were a few speed bumps along the way, but the smooth pavement always seemed to return, until now. I am lost, and even my new GPS is having trouble locating me.

The light at my intersection has changed from green to yellow to red a hundred times, a thousand times, and still I am stuck. The other traffic has stopped honking at me, and now passes me by, with only some curious glances from impatient drivers. They know I am not going anywhere and have learned to maneuver around me. I have become a landmark in my own right. The tow truck driver is tired of rescuing me, considering no matter where he takes me, I somehow wind up right back here at this damn intersection.

My clutch is not the only thing that is depressed. My mind and my tires are spinning, yet I still cannot get on solid ground. I think if I sit here much longer, some young vandals will remove my parts, and I will become a skeleton whose rusty frame will slowly disappear, like the bars on a swing set in the yard of children who have grown up and moved away, leaving only their childhood remnants behind.

I think I must need a tune-up, or some new spark plugs. My springs aren't bad, but the oil is a little thick, not as light and clear as it once was, now a slightly polluted version of its former self, like a salad dressing that has passed its expiration date by a year or two. Maybe I should have opted for the high octane gas rather than the less expensive one. My performance might have improved.

Sure, my tires are worn. They've seen a lot of miles, but there is some tread left. I just can't seem to get any traction.

Perhaps my windshield is dirty, blocking the view and preventing me from seeing where I am going. The washer fluid tank is full, but my wipers seem to be stuck. The back window is clear, so I know where I've been but don't want to go back.

So, with a body that made it through its last inspection, has a working engine, and lots of fuel, why do I remain glued to this pavement, like a piece of discarded chewing gum that has been run over and is now permanently adhered to the right hand lane?

It's got to be my transmission, a problem with my gears sticking. The lever is frozen and the force of my desire to shift will snap it off, and then there will be no hope at all. Not even Aamco will be able to salvage me.

No More Renewals

Relationships, like books, have beginnings, middles, and endings. With relationships, however, you don't always get to the end, leaving you in an emotional limbo. He was my book.

Now, I'm having this running argument with the librarian. She's telling me that I cannot have the book again, while I'm trying to explain to her that I haven't read the last chapter. I need to read the last chapter!

"Look," she tells me, her patience stretched thin like spandex on the morbidly obese, "you have had this book for almost two years, and it's been renewed seventeen times, not to mention all the overdue fines you've paid."

"Where does it say, in your list of library regulations, that there's a limit on renewals?" I ask, my voice catching on something I cannot swallow.

"There are other people who might want this book, and they can't read it if you're constantly renewing it," she chastises.

"Let's be honest. There are no other people who want this book. There's no waiting list. We're not talking about a bestseller here. I'm the only one with any interest in this story."

"Why don't you just go to Barnes and Noble and BUY the book?"

"I already checked. It's out of print and there's no way I can get a copy. Anyway, I don't really know if I want my own copy, I just want to know how the damn book ends!"

At this point, we're both holding onto a corner of the book, like two children in kindergarten arguing over a block they each claim to need in order to finish their toppling tower.

My hands are sweaty, my knuckles turning white with my efforts to keep possession. Is there a library referee to make a decision here?

"Why can't you finish the last chapter?" she asks quietly, beginning to soften at my pain.

"Because," I try to explain, "the book keeps getting longer. I can never get to the end. I'd be happy just to see the next page, just after where I left off."

I now realize the book is so heavy, I can barely hold onto it. If the librarian doesn't get a stronger grip, it will fall to the floor and scatter the dust motes that have taken refuge under the shelves of segregated genres.

Admittedly, it was the cover of the book that first appealed to me, even though I had no idea of what the story line was. I know about the whole "don't judge a book…" thing, but it was attractive in a way, a little worn, with a few dog-eared pages.

There were no starred reviews, no recommendations, no book-lists it was a part of. In truth, I was only the second person to even read the book, and the first person left no Cliff notes to help me figure it out. Of course, she wasn't able to figure it out either, so there would have been no point. The previous reader just dumped it in the book return.

And so, I remain rooted to this speckled gray library linoleum, thinking I will come back tomorrow with a pillow, a blanket, my toothbrush, my cholesterol medication, and live between the stacks, holding this book to my chest, slowly turning its pages until the type fades and I can no longer see.

Beware the Three Inch Font

Size does matter. Beware the big, bold font. As I grab the paper while my coffee cools, I hope the headlines will appear in letters less than three inches high, a subtle signal that the world is not about to end, a tsunami has not wiped out some poor population, or an earthquake has not split open some crowded country, casually dropping civilians and rusted cars into a concrete abyss. Two inch letters are tough, but three would be unbearable.

My hand trembles as the paper unfolds, revealing news of the world. We have gotten used to stories of corruption, murder, politicians gone awry. These tidbits warrant a mere one inch attention grabber. Two-inchers are a little tougher to take. Wars are escalating, children are suffering at the hands of abusers, religious radicals are shooting peaceful card-carrying protestors.

School bombings, assassinations, terrorists here and abroad, plane crashes. Those are the paper sellers, the screaming headlines, the three- inchers. They make us drop the coffee cup, put our hands to our chests, stop whatever we're doing to read the words that will shake us, albeit temporarily, to our core.

When you left, it was my personal three-inch headline. It rocked my world, and I was amazed that people continued to go to work, shopped for groceries, went to school. How could they, in light of this devastating development? Okay, it wasn't front page fodder, but it was earth shattering, nevertheless. To me. To me.

The Master of Minutiae

We lay in a bed, two parallel bodies, not touching, watching the ceiling fan slowly rotate its dusty blades. We hear the outdoor sounds of a dog left in a yard, barking pleadingly to be let back in, even on this warm, cloudy night. A stray cat is shrieking. Crickets are chirping for mates. Ah, the need to communicate.

Here we are, two humans with thousands of words to use, and nothing to say. We talk of the weather, the price of gas, the stock market. We converse in triviality, as if it were a language of its own.

We drive together in a car, looking ahead, discussing roads and routes, while our own paths are becoming divergent, going to separate destinations. We don't know this yet, and think we are on the same page, but that is true only on the map.

We fill the void with meaningless dialogue. We are walking on thin ice, and the wrong word will break that ice, tossing us into the cold depths below, so we tread carefully, using light weight words rather than the heavy, meaningful ones.

The things that should be said are left unspoken , and the lump in my throat is constricting my voice box. Why is it so hard? I have tried using the words that begin in my heart, but they float away and fall on deaf ears. They ring someplace else in the universe, but they do not ring for you. I think I am shouting them, but after so many attempts perhaps they are reduced to a whisper, and you no longer hear them. My throat is sore, my lips are parched, from repeated efforts. Please help me!

The Pool

We used to go swimming in that pool, years ago, both of us just kind of falling in at the same time. We splashed, frolicked, and dove together, moving seamlessly through the depths of chlorination. The days were warm and sunny, and we returned to the pool everyday. Although my skin was as wrinkled as crepe paper left over from a birthday party, I thought I'd stay in that pool forever, but one day you were gone and I was swimming solo. You were not to be found, though I frantically searched every corner of that concrete hole in the ground.

I beseeched lifeguards and other swimmers to help me find you, but you had completely vanished, as if the molecules of your body had turned to liquid and become part of the water we swam in. Perhaps you had been a mirage on a stifling, steamy day and, when I looked for you, you were gone.

Hoping for your return, I stayed in the water, but my raft had developed a small leak, and remaining afloat became more and more difficult. Frantically doggy paddling, I began to sink to the bottom, my eyes stinging from the chemicals and the tears. Who could distinguish?

The water cooled, the crowds thinned, and the pool was finally drained, and I was able to drag my weary body up the ladder and out. My skin was cold and clammy, and a great chill encased me. I went home to thaw, but vivid dreams of our swimming days together kept me from sleeping. You continued to exist in my night visions, but you were physically gone from my waking hours. I ached for you, unsure of your whereabouts.

You had buoyed me up for all that time and my body, as well as my fears, had become weightless. I was buoyant on bliss, high on happiness. We were the gold medal synchronized swimmers, moving together in unison. Others watched us and smiled. We were like two children, giddy with the newness of a just-made friend, but then you moved away without a word.

Life went back to what it was, but not really, and now winds whipped and leaves flew. Snow covered the earth and filled the pool. Another spring and summer came and went, and still I did not return to the water, and then another year, measured in increments of twelve flipped pages, went by.

In that following spring, you found me again and beckoned me to join you. You were ready to dive back in, take the plunge, and return to our carefree, happy days, but I was reticent, afraid of losing my breath. I was fearful of drowning in a place where even the tanned, toned lifeguards would not be able to save me. Frozen on the diving board, I looked down into that cold water and could not commit to making the jump. My knees shook, my heart pounded, my breath came in small, audible gasps. Tears streamed down my cheeks. If I didn't stop, the saline content of the water would rise ever so slightly, and algae would begin to grown between my toes.

I called to you and asked if we could first wade in the kiddy pool, test the waters, but you were adamant in your demands to return to the deep end. Too soon, I told you, too soon. I need to wet my feet and acclimate myself again to the feel of the water on my skin, the feel of your skin on mine.

You are gone again, and I am still standing here on this board. The lifeguards and the swimmers have departed, the pool is empty, and only a few leaves and dead bugs are in the bottom. It is time for me to get off, climb back down the diving board ladder, and return home. I will not come back to the pool again for, if I did, we would only pull each other down, drowning together in the depths of despair, our arms and legs intertwined, but I will keep you in my thoughts and wonder if you have returned each summer, or if you have moved on to another pool and another swimmer.

The Brass Ring

It was there, in plain sight, dangling at the end of the wooden arm that was painted red and white. The circus music of the carousel played different tunes as I used up all the tickets I had been allotted. I yearned for that shiny, cylindrical piece of metal that tempted me to reach beyond my grasp, almost falling off my wooden horse, my legs too short to reach the stirrups. My carved palomino was never in the right place at the right time. He was too high or too low, I was too tall or too short, to be able to grasp that tempting ring in my sweaty hand. My fingers strained, willing themselves to somehow lengthen at precisely the correct second, but they didn't make contact. Close, so close. Again and again.

I became fixated on that prize. The bystanders became a blur as I revolved, faster and faster. I tried to focus, but my eyes could not maintain contact, and the breeze from my momentum made them teary. Like a ballerina doing pirouettes, I tried to spot the ring, losing sight of it when I was on the other side, then regaining my focus for an instant, until it was gone.

As the ride slowed down, I thought, for sure, I would be able to grab the reward, but it continued to elude me. I would come back with more tickets, trying to perfect the necessary moves to attain my goal. The ticket seller gave me sympathetic looks as I put my dollars through the small slot, accepting a roll of yellow tickets in return. Other times, the tickets would be pink or blue, but it didn't matter. They were my chances for success.

Finally, on my twenty-seventh trip to the amusement park, I grabbed that ring! It was surprisingly cool to the touch, but I wasn't able to really study it until the ride slowed and stopped. Slightly dizzy from my concentrated efforts, I stumbled off the platform of ponies and poles, and peered at the treasure in my hand.

Upon closer inspection, it was not smooth and shiny, but rather rusty and pitted. Flakes of brass paint flecked off and scattered to the ground. It was a fake, a sham. I wanted my money back! As tears streamed down my flushed cheeks, it became more difficult to see what I had longed for. Perhaps the ring had never been authentic, or maybe it corroded while waiting for me to snatch it. Like an apple waiting on the branch, it had rotted to the core. Like sour grapes, maybe it had never been sweet at all.

Finding First Gear

Meteor Man

In my blue and white L.L Bean snowflake flannel paja-mas, and bare feet, I walked, transfixed, through the backdoor to examine a celestial object that had trav-eled light years to reach me. It was too hot to touch and blindingly bright, but I felt its power pulling on me, and knew my world would be forever altered.

Blazing through the black sky of a cold January night, a meteor had landed in my backyard with a bril-liance that illuminated my dark world. It set fire to my heart which had been frozen for years, melting it, and thawing my blood which began to course again through rigid veins.

My universe changed abruptly, and the blues and grays of my palette were instantly transformed into reds and yellows, colors that singed the stiff bristles of my brushes and turned them to ashes, like the glowing tip of a cigarette suddenly inhaled upon after a long absence from one's lips.

My feet were frozen to the ground, not because of the sub-zero temperature, but because of my incapacity to comprehend the enormity of what had just transpired. How could my neighbors still be asleep, unaware of the magnitude of this occurrence?

Thinking it was a dream, I returned to my bed and fell into a deep sleep, but woke up early, returning to the yard. The meteor, now a small, glowing rock, was still there and, donning my food-stained oven mitts, I picked it up and carried it into the house.

I lived alone now and there was no one to question me about the peculiar object I had placed upon a trivet, its little rubber feet resting on my worn Formica. The heat it emitted warmed my kitchen and I gazed upon it for hours, sipping my now cold coffee. After dressing and leaving the house to complete a myriad of mindless chores, I returned with some excitement to my rock. Unlike the coffee, it had lost none of its heat, and seemed even hotter than before.

Later that evening, upon retiring, my bed seemed cold, so I walked down the stairs, wrapped the rock in several kitchen towels and, carrying it, climbed back up the stairs, and put it next to me in bed. Even though it had looked huge upon its descent through the skies, it now fit easily into my hand. It had been a long time since there was something this warm sharing my blanket. During the night, I had stripped off my pajamas, and now found a small burn mark on my left breast. My sheets were damp with sweat.

My life continued as normal, rife with the business of family, friends, and jobs, but I now found myself spending more time at home and making up excuses for not going out. At first, people expressed concern but they, too, were busy with their own lives. My rock took on the significance of much more than an inanimate object, and I found myself consumed with it. The heat, as well as the contentment, lasted for over a year.

Slowly, ever so slowly, its heat began to dissipate. It not only became less blistering, but actually began to turn cold. Ice crystals formed in the slight cracks of its surface, yet it remained intact. I could no longer keep it in my bed, since I woke up frigid and shivering. The sheets were stiff, as if they had been hung damp on a line during a blustery, winter wind.

I feared that the life of my rock had run its course and I felt not only inconsolable disappointment, but a deep anger and resentment at the inherent promises it had implied. I was used, abandoned, and betrayed. I hated the rock. Despised it. Resented its very existence. Unwrapping it, I carried it downstairs, through the backdoor, and into the yard. With all the strength I had, I hurled that rock skyward, where it once again lit up the sky. It was a cad, a scoundrel, pretending to be something it was not.

It won't be back again. Its path will take it to other yards in other galaxies where it will glow brightly for a while, and then extinguish itself for good, totally spent, but leaving forever the faintest trail in the nighttime sky.

The Roller Coaster
and the Dead Man

I know, it sounds like a joke, the kind where you groan and roll your eyes. It's no joke. Believe me, it's no joke.

The dead man is on the ground in the amusement park, and I am kneeling next to him. The EMTs use a portable heart monitor, and the EKG line is flat. There are no ups and downs, no blips or squiggles, just one solid line. One small, beeping line than runs along the white paper, moving into nothingness. A crowd has formed and is growing, the curious and the bored, looking for adventure.

Of course, the really adventurous are on the roller coaster, hair flying, arms flailing, screaming loudly.

They don't yet notice the drama unfolding below their little speeding cars chugging up and flying down impossibly steep grades.

Oh, if that roller coaster had a heart, its EKG would be that of a heart attack victim, full of wild peaks and valleys, pointy "M"s and "V"s. The Alps, the Pyrenees, Mt. Everest!

Sometimes I think we have to make that relationship choice. After a while, those dizzy, nauseous thrill seekers on the wild rides seek the serenity of the flatliner. The flatliner, just before his eyes close for the final time, gazes longingly at that roller coaster and wishes he were on it. Oh, the irony of it all.

I feel like Goldilocks, sampling the fare of the Three Bears. Too hot, too cold, but not enough of the just right. Are we ever satisfied? If not, keep sampling until you find that happy medium without too many highs and lows, but just enough to keep life interesting.

Two Cookies on a Plate

One plate. Two cookies. One of them has wholesome ingredients, is healthy, has a nice shape to it, has a lovely sweetness, and is baked to perfection. The other cookie has inferior ingredients, is not nutritious, has an irregular shape, is slightly tart, and is over baked. A bit stale, you might say.

I've had both cookies before and know for a fact that the first cookie is delicious, puts a smile on my face, and has never caused a problem with my digestive system. The second cookie, on the other hand, leaves a bad aftertaste in my mouth, is not always pleasing, and upsets my stomach. So, why is it that I find my hand reaching for that second cookie? Where is my control? It reminds me of that Ouija board I played in high school, when I swore my hand wasn't moving the planchette at all, yet it continued to glide unwittingly under my trembling fingers.

I do this to myself. I choose the thing that is not good for me, that rots my teeth, plays havoc with my heart, bothers my bowels, and leaves me empty. I can have the more fulfilling treat that satisfies, the fresher one that won't let me down. Why don't I?

Perhaps I just need that challenge, like licking the bowl in which I've stirred the brownie mix, knowing the raw eggs could have salmonella. Like walking under the ladder. Like crossing the busy street after the little crossing icon has turned to red, tempting me to tempt my fate.

Sure, I can take a ride in a nice safe sedan, buckled up, but I longingly watch that fast motorcycle weaving quickly through traffic, and yearn to be on the back of it, my arms wrapped around the helmetless daredevil in the front, throwing caution to the wind.

After a slight case of salmonella poisoning, a small motorcycle accident, a near-miss crossing the street, a ladder falling on my head, I am much more cautious now. I want the healthy cookie, the things that are best for me.

So, why am I once again reaching for the cookie that is better left on the plate?

Cloning

After you had left, I was doing one of those spring-cleaning purges, changing quilts, flipping the mattress, and dusting in those places that do not often see the can of Pledge. There it lay on one of the lower slats of wood at the head of the bed frame. One small hair curled up as if in hibernation. I picked it up with the tip of my slightly sweaty pinky.

As I studied that small hair, I thought about cloning. What if I could take that tiny relic from your body and make it into a new you? You would, once again, be back in my life and in my bed, your head on the pillow next to mine. Ah, the possibilities of science. After all, they cloned sheep and created babies in test tubes. Why not you?

While I rubbed that thin strand between my fingers, I thought how a clone is an exact replica, the same DNA, the same traits. It would be the same YOU, the you who had hurt me, broken my heart, turned my pillow case into a sponge, absorbing the tears that freely flowed from my red-rimmed eyes.

Why in the world would I want to make another one of you, to hurt me again, or some other poor, unsuspecting victim, unaware at first of your cold side, your disappearing acts, your callous, shallow self?

I took that hair and, like a dead goldfish, flushed it down the toilet, watching it swirl clockwise around and around until it was gone. I washed my hands and went back to dusting and found another hair.

I put it into an envelope to save, just in case.

The Pound

He's looking at me with those moist, brown eyes, his mouth slightly open, exuding the merest hint of stale breath. His nose is pushing up against the cold bars of the cage. He wants to come home with me, but we've tried that arrangement before and I don't know if I'm up to the challenge and, believe me, it was a challenge.

I had found him abandoned, flea-bitten and forlorn, mangy and meek, undernourished and under desired. He followed me home and I provided the necessary comforts while searching for someone he belonged to. His owner, actually, was known to me, but she no longer wanted him. I wasn't sure if I did either, and this was not something I had even thought about. An instant companion in my newly solitary life was not in the plans. So much for plans.

As time went on, we fell into a comfortable co-existence, laced with affection and a kind of love. In a strange symbiotic way, we needed and depended upon each other. He was gentle and loving, and we spent many nights snuggling together on the couch. Bolder he became as his energy improved and he now bounded up the stairs to lie on my bed.

One night, when I returned home late, he growled at me, his upper lip curled in a meanness I had never seen before, but he calmed down shortly. Life returned to its usual easiness. Before long, however, he bit my hand as I reached for him. The bite was superficial, but it startled and angered me. I brought him downstairs and put him into the bathroom. When I went back to check on him, he was contrite, his tail between his legs. He licked my face and whimpered softly.

He disappeared for a week. Although it was still cool, the nights were above freezing, but I still worried constantly. The ads for a missing pet were never answered, but suddenly he returned. He acted as if nothing had happened, but there was a difference now, an invisible schism in our relationship.

I began to wonder if I had done something to scare him, perhaps something his previous owner had done. Now, my actions were controlled and slow, so as not to frighten him again. My confidence returned and I was no longer leery. Our truce was rudely broken, however, when he bit me again, this time drawing blood and requiring stitches.

The trust was now gone and I realized he could no longer stay with me. Not wanting to impose his short temper on an acquaintance, I hesitantly brought him to the pound. I couldn't watch as he was led to a cage, his head down, his tail dragging, and a low moan emitting from his throat. A low moan was emitting from my throat also, but it was drowned out by the din of the cage-filled room.

After I arrived back home, I could not stop crying. The house was quiet and empty, and I began putting the dog paraphernalia away, not yet sure if it was destined for the dump or the Goodwill store. Perhaps some young child with a new pet would be able to use the items. For now, they went into the back of a closet and then were forgotten, but not really.

At odd moments, I would think of my canine companion and wonder if he were still at the pound, if he had been adopted, or, worse, if he had been euthanized. At random moments, there would be a catch in my throat when I heard or saw a similar dog. It reminded me of the days when I had breastfed my babies and, years later, hearing another baby would make my breasts ache with the tenderness of unexpressed milk.

I had considered getting another dog, and did, in fact, dog-sit for a friend. Once burned, it was hard to imagine setting myself up for the hurt and mistrust, but I was lonely.

Many months later, when a chore brought me to the neighborhood where the pound was located, I went in, much against my better judgment. After inquiring, I was told that, indeed, he was still there, languishing. It broke my heart to see him there but, when he saw me, he barked loudly and his tail did a dance of its own accord, brushing the walls of his small enclosure.

Now, I am standing in front of that cage unsure of the next step. Do I dare risk the pain, physical and emotional, of continuing this relationship? Has he changed? Can you really teach an old dog new tricks? The tears are flowing down my face and, when I bend down, he licks them away, his small pink tongue on my cheeks, my eyes, my mouth.

Yes, I will take him back. I know he will continue to hurt me, but he breaks my heart and I cannot abandon him again. Maybe, in time, he will learn to trust. Maybe I will, too. Until then, I will love him, but will remember the fear of the past and will keep a part of me locked up and guarded. A sad basis for a relationship, but I am a sucker for second chances. Always have been, always will be.

Expiration Date

I was the short woman always leaning precariously into the refrigerated section in the back of the supermarket, checking the expiration date of the milk. My arms, extended to their fullest, reached to the remote rear of the drippy shelf, hoping to find a later date than the one stamped on the cartons in the front. There were times, calf muscles stretched achingly, I almost fell in from leaning too far, but one can never be careful enough to get the freshest possible carton. The same with eggs, cans, bread. Checking, checking, always checking.

With all the care that I put into checking when things would turn stale or sour, liquid or limp, how could I not have known that the relationship I was in had its own expiration date? How did that fact escape my meticulous attention to detail? I missed the curdles forming, the telltale odor of something rotting, deteriorating.

There was no date stamped on your forehead, no plastic piece attached to your wrist with a month and year. Nothing obvious. I had assumed your freshness was meant to last a long time. Like the plug-in room freshener in the dining room, the loss of the aroma was so subtle and slow, my nose did not pick up the signs of its decreasing effectiveness.

Maybe there were tiny, telltale signs, or perhaps there were signs that were hitting me in the head with the force of a hurricane or jackhammer, pounding away, that I chose to ignore. I was a teenager with headphones, totally oblivious to the world around me.

If there is a next time, I will analyze more precisely, sniff more, get new reading glasses, and check those clues. The answer does not always lie within the parameters you rely on, but can jump up and bite you in the ass. So warned.

Shifting Into Second

Safety Nets

In thirty years, the trapeze artist had not once used the net billowing below him, but when he did not see it there, he was paralyzed with such fear that he could no longer walk from one end of the wire to the other. He remained frozen on his platform, incapable of taking even a baby step.

The young girl could easily swim two laps in the pool, going from the shallow end to the deep, and back again. The small inflatable bands on her upper arms were not necessary anymore, but when her father forgot to blow them up and fasten them around her moist skin, she could not take one single stroke in the water, even though she had done it countless times before.

Pedaling madly on his new, neon blue bike, the boy no longer needed his training wheels and, in fact, never actually let them touch the ground now that his balance had improved, but when his big brother used the Allen wrench to remove them, he was unable to ride to the bottom of the driveway, so petrified was he of falling down.

When I told my lover, after years of a roller coaster ride, that I was leaving the amusement park, no longer amused, I could barely utter the words, even though I had said them to myself and gained a new independence I had not felt before.

Oh, the nets we weave, both literal and figurative, the real ones and the imagined, the ones we need and the ones we only think we need. We practice for years to get to the point where we can do it by ourselves and yet, when we actually must, we recoil in fear, doubting our ability to do so. We are standing on the edge of the diving board, our toes curled, looking down into water we have looked down into countless times before and, for an instant, we cannot jump on that board and let it release us, headfirst, into a rectangle filled with clear liquid. We can't jump out of a plane, we can't jump out of a relationship, we can't even jump in place.

My friend and I hug, tightly, more tightly than we did when we were still together. Every beginning starts from the closure of something else. It does. It does. We'll jump together, you and I, holding hands, into the un-known and, halfway down, we'll let go and continue on our separate journeys, not saying we can't meet again and hold hands for part of the long walk into the rest of our lives. Or not.

Musical Chairs

We were walking faster and faster, bumping into the little chairs with our short legs, knocking some an inch or two out of their neat, back-to-front formation. The music was playing, some fast little tune known to all of us, possibly "Ring Around the Rosie" or "Pop Goes the Weasel." After the song had been on for mere seconds, our as yet unbroken hearts were racing, pounding in our little, pre-pubescent chests, as our fingers intentionally brushed the sturdy wooden seats we were circling, staking our claim. Our adrenalin pumping, we tried to anticipate when the music would suddenly stop. False starts were made, and we had to get our little fannies into one of the chairs at precisely the right second, or risk not having a chair.

There was a sense of dread we had felt as children. We knew one of us would not have a seat when the music stopped. Someone would have to leave the game, knowing another would be the winner. We might have been at a birthday party, our pointy little hats stuck upon our heads with a thin piece of elastic, nearly choking us, or in gym class, still too young to emit a sweaty aroma, but, nonetheless, with damp, little palms. Perhaps we were in our kindergarten class, our teacher watching as we marched quickly in our polished saddle shoes, admonishing us to play fairly.

Now, we are the adults with no referee to insure the fairness of what we are doing.

Oh, it doesn't even matter what the chairs are like anymore. Some have worn, stained upholstery, others have springs visibly sticking up through tattered fabric, others replete with cat hair. Some are overstuffed, with and without arms, one even missing a leg, another barely having a seat where the cane has pulled through the little holes on the circumference. We're a lot heavier now, and the wooden chairs are gone. It doesn't matter. Any seat is better, in our minds, than no seat at all.

Please, we silently wish, don't let it be me. I'll take any chair, as long as I still have one. Don't make me be the only one without a seat, shamed by my aloneness.

We are divorced, widowed, separated, single, but we still, in some way, want to have a seat to support us. As the remaining available seats dwindle in number, we feel a desperation that there will be none left. Even a folding, temporary chair will do.

It's like the fraternity mixers in college where every male and female paired off, leaving you standing by the bar, hoping someone, anyone, would come up to you and start to talk or ask you if you'd like a beer. As the hour got later, even the short ones, the fat ones, the acne-scarred ones started looking taller, thinner, clear-skinned.

Now the seasons pass quickly, old calendars are discarded for new ones, and we are beginning to panic. We see only the couples, out jogging, having coffee, at a concert. We fixate on them, not noticing the singles in the world. Like young women trying to conceive, we notice only the pregnant people, wondering what is wrong with us.

Feeling panic and despair, you decide to try and find a chair. You're like a baby-boomer Goldilocks, and try them all. The big stuffed ones hurt your back, the old ones make your skin itch, the broken ones stab you with their shards and, suddenly, you realize you don't want a chair at all! You're fine the way you are, and don't need some old discard to give you support. Maybe, in the future, some fine seat will be vacated, and you will be in the right place at the right time to jump into it. But, if that day doesn't come, you are still good and strong, capable and independent.

Flypaper

I was stuck, literally and figuratively. Not only was I stuck on the paper, I was stuck to it. Parts of me were coming off, and every time I tried to pull away, another bit of me was lost. I wondered what would remain in the end. Fly remnants. Musca domestica, if you want to be formal.

Not only was the paper sticky, it had an allure that was difficult to resist. It was a combination of aroma and the innate quality of the paper itself, a kind of iridescence that was both glossy and matte at different times. The shine would attract me, like a moth to light, and other times the very dull finish of the matte would bore me, even repulse me. The paper, like a chameleon, could change at will. It was like the poles of a spinning magnet, now attracting, now repelling.

The other flies were not attracted to this trap, and continued to buzz freely, continuing on their way. They were surviving in their wisdom. What, in my compound eye view of the world, did I see in this paper? Why did I keep going back to it, then try to get away? I had never considered myself to be a masochistic little creature, but here I was torturing myself, mentally and physically, not to mention emotionally.

My antennae must have been functioning below capacity, since I was not able to use them properly to ward off the inherent danger. They were not picking up the warning signals and relaying them to my wings. Fly, fly away home. Apparently, I was not using much sense at all. My small, three-part body was being controlled by a primitive heart rather than by a small brain. My wings were becoming clipped, and it was harder to escape.

I used to pride myself on my innate intelligence, pretty good for a fly. Where had I gone wrong by letting myself become attracted to this artificial lure? It was like a sweet dessert in the Venus fly trap. I knew it was there, knew it was a risky gamble, and I could not control my appetite for it. So there I was, buzzing around that damn, sticky flypaper! So much for my membership in Mensa and my high IQ - insect quotient.

Now I am pulling off each of my six little legs, one at a time, which is no easy task. I persevere, however, and finally, for a brief moment, become free. No longer totally intact, I do my best to regain my strength and resist the lure for good. I cannot make any promises, but each day finds me stronger in my resolve.

The Broken Ballerina

I was a virtuoso, the princess of pirouettes. As I spun, it was necessary to spot, and with each revolution, you were my spot, the thing I would focus on to prevent dizziness. You were there, and my eyes would connect, albeit briefly, with yours. Always there, always there, until the time they weren't.

Scanning the room, my gaze frantically searched for you with each turn. I began to feel lightheaded and was losing my momentum and equilibrium. Objects and colors blurred like clothes spinning randomly in a laundromat dryer. With my balance compromised, I could not continue.

I would not yet give up, however, and practiced, day after day, my leg upon the barre. With every ounce of endurance, I stretched my limbs, leaning this way and that. Muscles tore and still I stretched further and further, beyond anything I had done before. My toes were pointed, my thighs and calves burning. Begrudgingly, I removed my leg from the wooden pole and placed it gingerly back on the floor.

Later, I tried again. Donning my toe shoes, I stretched, my body taut, muscles aching. The support in the shoes was gone, as if it had been gnawed away by little mice during my dancing hiatus, and pain seared through my feet, no longer protected by the padding. One by one, my toes broke, and I could only hobble across the stage.

I was like the little ballerina in a music box who would spring to life when the top was raised, twirling in time to the wound up notes. My tutu was pink, and covered the hips of my plastic torso, but now the top of the box was closed and the pink tulle was tattered and faded. No longer did lilting melodies play while I danced my heart out. As if in a coffin, I thought I would forever remain in my music box tomb.

My arms, once graceful, were now stiff. Fingers that had been beautifully flexed were now gnarled and crooked. Limbs that were limber became cramped and wasted. Like a sleeping beauty, I waited for that lid to be lifted. I could hear the music in my heart, but that, too, became fainter and more distant.

One day, in the future, the music returned, ever so slightly, notes so soft I could not be sure I had actually heard them. Gradually, they became louder and louder and, as if on cue, my muscles relaxed, my fingers un-curled, and my toes flexed in a newfound gracefulness. My eyes opened and I saw that my costume was new. I gingerly stepped out of my music box prison and re-turned to the real world once again.

Too much time had elapsed, however, and I knew I could no longer be the ballerina I had been. I tossed the toe shoes, discarded the tutu, and removed the ballet barre from the wall. I would find an alternative passion in which, for the time being, I did not need to rely on anyone else. And, I did, and my heart soars again.

Sightseeing at Home

The sheer magnitude of the Grand Canyon was so amazing, it brought tears to my eyes and left me speechless. My mind could not wrap itself around the enormity of the chasm, and I was hanging on to the edge. Unfortunately, I was not in Arizona, but rather on the edge of my queen size bed in the master bedroom. My traveling companion, who I had thought would accompany me on all life's journeys, was on the other side. The canyon was between us, lurking dangerously beneath the flannel sheets. Even the down comforter could not provide enough warmth to protect us from the frigid temperatures.

I tried to touch him, but the distance was so wide that my arms could not reach. The night was so dark, he could not see the trail of tears glistening on my cheeks. The noise of the silence was so loud it was deafening, and he could not hear my whispered pleas. For yet another night, I cried myself to sleep, my arms wrapped around myself, trying to protect my body from falling into the abyss below.

I was a remnant of a table setting gone awry. No longer was there spooning, and my bowl was empty, my plate smashed on the rocks below. My knife, no longer sharp, could not cut the tension in the room. Even the tines of my fork had gone their separate ways, making another utterly useless utensil.

Like the erosion that formed the canyon itself, our weathering, too, took time. Many years had worn down the bonds between us. Like two lonely bricks, our mortar was gone and there was nothing left to keep us together. The bonds had dried up and cracked. Even Crazy Glue could not mend us. We were the Humpty Dumpty set, fractured beyond repair. We were the pieces of a jigsaw puzzle purchased at a garage sale, too many of us gone to make a coherent picture. Never again would we be complete.

It would be impossible to mark the beginning of the end. There were many beginnings, I suppose, each a hairline crack into which miniscule molecules of water would hide, then freeze and expand, crumbling the rock and breaking it apart. The acidity of the water, too, increased its weathering action. The early soft breezes had turned to occasional gusts, and the seeds of promising starts had begun to be blown away, like tumbleweed on the prairie.

Our erosion was quiet, not accompanied by loud noises or harsh movements, rather like a silent glacier creeping along and changing everything in its path. It took its own sweet time, moving randomly, just the way those things go. Moving on, moving on.

Well, I guess I just didn't want to be a tourist anymore. I had seen enough sights with my traveling companion and it made me lonely. If, at some later time I decided to travel again, it would be by myself, open to new adventures. If a kind tour group scooped me up into its embrace, that would be fine. If not, my own adventures would suffice on this journey we call life.

The Acupuncturist's Dilemma

My eyes were closed as I lay on the examining table, needles protruding perpendicularly from my damp skin. I was trying to shut out external stimuli to focus on the therapy at hand, but the sloshing sound of water immediately told my ears to send an electronic message to open my eyes. I screamed.

The nurse who rapidly entered my small room had her jaw hanging as she nervously appraised the situation. Her white-stockinged feet, ensconced firmly in the professional white clogs, were submerged in two inches of liquid, and she quickly exited to find the doctor. Fortunately, the rubber soles prevented her from slipping on the way and having to doggy paddle to the door.

When both the nurse and the doctor, as well as the curious receptionist, came running into my room, the sight that greeted them resembled a garden hose, the kind with little evenly spaced holes to water the lawn. Unfortunately, I was the hose and a clear liquid was oozing through the holes in my skin where the needles dotted my derma.

After years of difficult relationships that led to migraines, weight gain, and an overall sense of melancholy, my doctors, including general practitioners, allergists, and psychologists, gently persuaded me to try acupuncture since traditional remedies had proved ineffective.

Now, in a last ditch effort, I was nonchalantly watering the plants in the room, as well as the wallpaper. Without the aid of an umbrella, the acupuncturist and the nurse began quickly to remove the needles and, slowly, the mysterious liquid sprouting from my body began to stop. A little bit of it was put into a syringe for immediate analysis.

While the testing began, I was moved into another room, told to dry off, and offered a clean gown to put on. By now, I was shivering from cold and sheer panic. Oddly enough, I felt lighter as I slowly slid onto the new, dry examining table, where the roll of paper at the head of the table was not saturated, and its cool crispness made a crackling sound as I lay down, perplexed and exhausted.

When the results were in, I was gently told by the nurse to relax, get dressed, sit up, and wait for the doctor. She once again took my blood pressure, which was lower than it had been in years, and weighed me. She was amazed that I had lost twenty pounds since I had stepped on the scales an hour earlier.

Although it seemed an eternity, it was only a few minutes until the acupuncturist reappeared with his clipboard and test results. He informed me that the liquid had a very high salt concentration, but no bacteria. He was baffled and his many years of experience were no help to him in determining the cause of the odd phenomenon that had just occurred.

Yet, I knew! I knew! I had been purged of my years of unshed tears, gallons of sadness I was not able to express. I would trade in my murky saltwater for that of a crystal clear lake, and sail into new beginnings. Bon voyage, self!

Barnacles

They're clinging to my side, slowing my forward motion and causing drag as I plod through the briny waves. Attached with the power of a marine superglue, they hug my hull with the tenacity of an octopus. If they are scraped off, they magically reappear, stronger and more stubborn.

Sometimes, they all leave at once, like rats following the Pied Piper. Other times, they are back tenfold and they impede my smooth sailing, compromising the aerodynamics of my shell. When they are knocked off, they pull part of my protective finish away, letting rot into my inner core. I am left with no protection and my once youthful sheen is weathered and aging.

Get a grip on yourself! Get those damned things off once and for all. These cancerous crustaceans are draining the life out of me. Clinging, clinging, holding on for dear life. Let go, you nasty calcareous shells. Fall off, you freeloading hitchhikers. I am sick of your lecherous attachment to me. You are draining every bit of my energy and strength. You sappy little suckers, find your own ride through these stormy seas. Put out your little thumbs and get yourselves another ride. Oh, wait, you don't have thumbs, do you? Worry not, I'll flag down a maritime checkered cab for you, calcium derivatives.

Once, proud and sleek, I sliced through those waves. The higher, the better, no challenge too big. Hurricane seas? Bring them on! Tsunamis? Yes, yes! My smooth, clean, waxed surface offered no resistance to the salty seas. My wake was vast, spreading in a "v" formation behind me, like the geese of fall, flying off to warmer waters, tropical destinations.

Like a faint freckle, that first barnacle appeared on my skin, barely noticed. Soon, he was joined by his whole damn extended family, all moving in, crowding each other. Underwater U-Hauls. The crazy aunts, the senile grandfathers, the psychotic kids, the mangy dogs, the clawing cats. Clawing, clawing. Leave me alone, pathetic parasites. Get your own lives and leave mine alone. Next, the whole neighborhood joined them, lured by the promise of a free ride. They were the slums on my sides.

One by one, those chagrined barnacles disentangled themselves. I could not contain my mirth as they fell off and slowly floated to the bottom of the sea. They crumbled and broke on their way down, slowly dissolving into nothingness, becoming a part of the water. As the last of them fell, I slowly gained speed, my throttle open, heading for the open seas.

No more would I be subject to the leeches, the hangers on. Like the snail with the smallest shell, I rid myself of encumbrances. I would sail freely, plotting a life-long journey, perhaps picking up a passenger for part of the ride.

Perhaps not.

The Speed Bump

What the hell was that? Here I am, cruising along, minding my own business, when my car lurches up in the air and comes down again on the other side of an enormous, bright yellow speed bump that someone must have inadvertently left in the middle of the road! How could I have missed it?

I'm normally a very observant, careful driver, and here I am totally caught off guard by something I should have seen coming. After all, I'm not a new driver and have quite a few miles under my belt.

The next time I'm out, on the same road, wouldn't you know it, I run into that same damn speed bump! My car not only bounces up in the air again, but lands hard with my exhaust system hanging urgently from the bottom of my undercarriage. Now the bump is a little harder to cross with all the paraphernalia sagging on the cement.

Weeks later, a bit preoccupied, as usual, that same speed deterrent rises up to wreak havoc once again. This is ridiculous, a waste of time and money, not to mention an extreme embarrassment. My vehicle and my emotions are severely maimed.

As I'm dragging my vehicle to the service station, it suddenly dawns on me that there is a simple solution. Drive on an another road, honey, ditch those bumps and obstacles. Reroute, recharge, head into the future on a newly paved highway, and don't look back.

Barbara Wood

is a retired teacher who spent thirty-three years teaching first grade at School 18 in Troy, New York. She enjoys reading, designing, exploring different avenues of creativity, volunteering, and trying new adventures. She has been involved with writing and the arts since she was a child.

When life took some unexpected turns, she turned to writing to explore the varied interactions between people, and hopes these short stories will be meaningful to anyone who has ever been in a relationship.

She is the mother of three grown children and resides in Troy, New York.